FINDING AN IDENTITY: EARLY AMERICA AND THE COLONIAL PERIOD 1492–1774

ALEX WOOLF

CHELSEA HOUSE
An Infobase Learning Company

FINDING AN IDENTITY: EARLY AMERICA AND THE COLONIAL PERIOD 1492–1774
Copyright © 2011 Bailey Publishing Associates Ltd

Produced for Chelsea House by Bailey Publishing Associates Ltd, 11a Woodlands, Hove BN3 6TJ, England

Library of Congress Cataloging-in-Publication Data
Woolf, Alex, 1964-
  Finding an identity : early America and the Colonial Period, 1492-1774 / Alex Woolf.
    p. cm. — (A cultural history of women in America)
  Includes index.
  ISBN 978-1-60413-927-3
  1. Women—United States—History—17th century. 2. Women—United States—History—18th century. I. Title.
  HQ1416.W676 2011
  305.40973'0903—dc22
                        2010029225

Project management by Patience Coster
Text design by Jane Hawkins
Picture research by Shelley Noronha
Printed and bound in Malaysia
Bound book date: April 2011

10 9 8 7 6 5 4 3 2 1

The publishers would like to thank the following for permission to reproduce their pictures:
The Art Archive: 6, 9 (Culver Pictures), 26 (Culver Pictures), 50 (W. Langdon Kihn/NGS Image Collection); The Bridgeman Art Library: 10 (Private Collection), 13 (Gift of James E. Scripps), 14 (Gift of Mrs. J. Maxwell Moran/Buffalo Bill Historical Center, Cody, Wyoming), 16 (Edward Ingersoll Brown Fund), 18 (Private Collection), 21 (Bequest of Ward Nicholas Boylston, 1828), 28 (Private Collection), 29 (Collection of the New York Historical Society, USA), 30 (Private Collection), 31 (Peter Newark American Pictures), 33 (Ken Welsh), 34 (Collection of the New York Historical Society, USA), 36 (Private Collection), 45 (Peter Newark American Pictures), 52 (Newberry Library, Chicago, Illinois, USA), 53 (Virginia Historical Society, Richmond, Virginia, USA), 54 (Virginia Historical Society, Richmond, Virginia, USA), 55 (The Stapleton Collection), 59 (Collection of the New York Historical Society, USA); Charleston Historical Society: 25; Corbis: 5 (© Burstein Collection), 8 (© Bettmann), 24 (© Bettmann), 27 (© Burstein Collection), 35 (Rykoff Collection), 37 (© Bettmann), 38 (Lebrecht Music & Arts), 39 (© Bettmann), 41 bottom (© Bettmann), 44, 46 (Tim Wright), 47 (© Bettmann), 48 (Richard T. Nowitz); Getty Images: 20, 42, 43 (Hulton Archive), 49, 56, 57; Maryland State Art Collection: 23; North Wind Picture Archive: 17 (AKG), 41 top (AKG); TopFoto: 58; TopFoto/The Granger Collection: 7, 11, 12, 15, 22, 32, 51.

CONTENTS

THIS BOOK LOOKS AT THE EARLY HISTORY of women in the land that would become the United States of America. It covers the period from the time of the European discovery of the Americas near the end of the 15th century to the eve of the American War of Independence in 1774. For nearly half of that period, practically the only women in the continent were Native Americans. White European women did not arrive in any numbers in North America until the early 17th century. The first African slaves—men and women—arrived there at about the same time.

Much has been written about this period of American history—most of it concerning the activities of explorers, landowners, merchants, political leaders, and military commanders—all of them men. Much less has been written about the other half of the population. The challenge for any historian writing about women in early America and the colonial period is the scarcity of primary sources. Few white women wrote anything down. As for black and Native American women, virtually no personal accounts of their lives exist.

Historians must look instead for references to women in books, letters, and journals written by men. They can study paintings, clothing, jewelry, and other artifacts. Official documents, such as ship passenger lists, court records, and wills, can also be helpful. Using these clues, historians can form a fairly accurate picture of women's lives during the period. As to the details of their *inner* lives—their thoughts, ideas, hopes, and dreams—about these we can only speculate.

Right: The lives of women during this period were mainly devoted to raising children and looking after the home. They passed these domestic skills on to their daughters.

MANAGING THE HOME

"*In the management of household affairs the husband leaves everything to the wife and never interferes.*"

Settlement worker David Zeisberger, a missionary living among the Lenni Lenape (the Delaware), c. 1760

CHAPTER I

THE EARLY YEARS

THE 17TH AND 18TH CENTURIES WERE A TIME OF CULTURAL CLASHES and upheaval in North America as three peoples—native, European, and African—uncomfortably coexisted. Europeans came with plans to settle and trade, but as they grew in confidence, the nature of their project changed to one of exploitation and conquest. Native Americans had little choice but to adapt to and occasionally confront this encroachment. As for the Africans, their enforced deportation to the New World left them virtually stripped of their culture, and the shackles of slavery grew ever tighter during the period.

Above: This painting depicts Christopher Columbus's landing in the New World on October 12, 1492. His discovery marked the beginning of the European colonization of the Americas.

THE NATIVE EXPERIENCE

When the first Europeans set foot in the New World toward the end of the 15th century, there were between 10 and 20 million Native Americans living in North America. They were organized around extended clans or tribes, of which there were at least 300 scattered throughout the continent. The men of these tribes occupied themselves with hunting, warfare, and trade. Their main role was to defend their families against attack from rival tribes and hunt animals for food. The women were responsible for raising the children and feeding, clothing, and sheltering their families. With the men often away from home, women exercised a great deal of control over their lives and enjoyed a high status within the tribe.

EUROPEAN DISEASES

The arrival of the Europeans had a devastating impact on the native population. The Europeans brought diseases with them, such as influenza, measles, and smallpox, to which the Native Americans had no immunity. It is estimated that during the first 100 years of European contact, the native population of eastern North America declined by between a half and two-thirds as a result of disease. Native Americans also suffered enslavement, malnutrition, wars, and massacres as well as a steady loss of their lands, particularly at the hands of English colonists.

BENEFITS

European contact did, however, bring some beneficial changes. From French explorers seeking food and furs, the Iroquois and Algonquian peoples of Canada obtained firearms, blankets, metal, and cloth. In the Great Lakes region, the Huron people's alliance with the French in the 1650s saved them from annihilation by the Iroquois.

GENDER ROLES

All these changes, good and bad, distorted the internal workings of the tribes, often affecting traditional gender roles. As the tribal elders died out, the collective knowledge of history and ceremony was lost. As women rejected suitors disfigured by disease, the birthrate declined. Some women married and had families with colonists, and on occasion they acted as intermediaries between the colonists and the tribes.

HUNTERS AND NOMADS

Europe's enormous demand for furs forced Native American men to spend increasing amounts of time away from home, hunting beaver, marten, and fox, and compelled tribes to move around in search of good hunting grounds. Settled farming tribes of the east coast became nomadic, disrupting traditional lifestyles of women, which were based around the home and the village. Instead of growing food for the family, women became preoccupied with the scraping, dressing, and trimming of furs for sale.

THE COLONIES

The first successful English colony in North America was Jamestown, Virginia, in 1607, followed by Plymouth Colony, founded in 1620 at Cape Cod Bay. At first, men dominated these colonies, but the female

Below: An Iroquois woman grinds corn into cornmeal. Traditional Native American lifestyles came under severe threat during the period.

TURNING POINT

THE HORSE

In the 16th century, Europeans introduced the horse to North America. The animal was adopted by Native Americans of the Great Plains, transforming their culture. It enabled them to hunt game—especially bison—more effectively, expand their territory, exchange goods with neighboring tribes, and carry out raids.

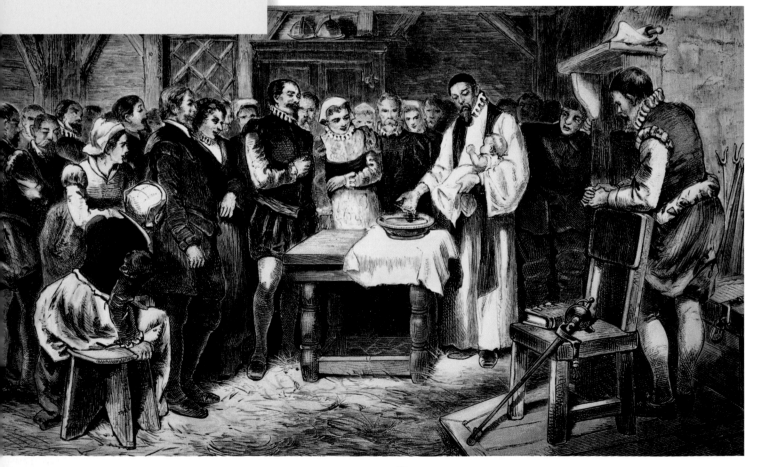

BREAKTHROUGH BIOGRAPHY

VIRGINIA DARE (1587–?)

In July 1587, 117 English settlers landed at Roanoke Island in present-day North Carolina with hopes of establishing a colony there. Less than a month after landing, one of the settlers, Ellinor Dare, gave birth to a daughter, Virginia—the first English child to be born in the New World. When she was nine days old, Virginia's grandfather, the colonists' governor John White, sailed back to England to seek assistance for the colony. When White returned in 1591, the colony had completely disappeared. Nothing is known of the fate of Virginia Dare or her fellow colonists.

population increased as women were lured across the Atlantic by better prospects of marriage and a home in the growing communities.

A STRUGGLE FOR SURVIVAL

In these early decades of colonial America, life was a struggle for survival for both men and women. The deeply held religious views of the settlers dictated that women should be subordinate to their husbands. Unlike their Native American counterparts, settler women had few rights or opportunities. Their lives were entirely dedicated to child rearing and domestic work.

THE WEALTHY EAST

The English steadily colonized the Atlantic seaboard from French Acadia to Spanish Florida. By the 1690s, most of eastern North America from Canada to the Mexican Gulf had been colonized by the French and English. The English colonial empire consisted of 12 colonies extending along the Atlantic seaboard. A thirteenth, Georgia, was

Below: The baptism of Virginia Dare. The girl's status as the first English child born in America transformed her into an almost-mythical figure.

founded in 1733. By this time, the east coast colonies were centered on well-ordered, thriving cities. Wealthy gentlewomen, dressed in the latest European fashions, hosted tea parties, and cooked fancy dishes. On the frontier to the west, life remained harsh. Women here tilled and harvested and, if necessary, defended their properties with a gun.

SLAVES FROM AFRICA

The first Africans to be brought to English North America arrived in Jamestown in 1619. They were regarded not as slaves but indentured servants (laborers under contract for a fixed term), and several won their freedom. Attitudes changed later in the 17th century as the economic advantages of slave owning became apparent. Slavery spread rapidly through the colonies, particularly in the South. Female slaves worked side by side with men in the fields. In the late 17th and early 18th century, slave codes were introduced, making it harder for slaves to win their freedom and prohibiting interracial marriage. By 1750, slavery was legal and widely practiced in all 13 of Britain's American colonies.

WAR AND REVOLUTION

From 1689, Britain fought a series of wars with France for control of the North American continent. The wars ended in 1763 with victory for Britain. Under the Treaty of Paris, Britain received almost all French territory in Canada and east of the Mississippi River and also Florida from Spain (France's ally). Britain now had control of the whole continent east of the Mississippi.

But Britain's domination was not as complete as it hoped: there were rumblings of discontent in its 13 original colonies. The colonists were unhappy at paying taxes to the British government without representation in the British Parliament. Barely a decade after Britain's victory in the wars against France, the first shots were fired in a revolutionary war that would end British rule in the 13 colonies and result in the establishment of an independent United States of America.

Above: A slave auction in the Dutch colony of New Amsterdam (present-day New York) in 1643. Slaves, newly arrived from Africa, would be inspected by potential buyers, then sold to the highest bidder.

TURNING POINT

THE AMERICAN REVOLUTION

The ideas of liberty and natural rights that underpinned the American Revolution would have a profound impact on American society, including its women. Many women began to recognize they could have a role to play in the new nation beyond the traditional one of wife and mother.

CHAPTER 2

DAILY LIFE

IN 1608, THE FIRST 150 WOMEN ARRIVED IN THE FLEDGLING COLONY of Jamestown, Virginia. They had been brought there by the Virginia Company, a group of London businessmen who hoped to profit from their investments in the New World. For the women in the newly established colonies, life must have amounted to never-ending drudgery. The shortage of labor meant that women would often work beside their husbands in the fields, but their primary sphere of responsibility was in the home.

> ## " FAMILY TIES
>
> "[The men] uppon esteeminge Virginia, not as a place of habitation butt only of a short sojourninge: have applied themselves and their labors wholly to the raysinge of present profitt, and utterly neglected . . . the verie necessities of Mans liffe. . . . Wee therfore judginge itt a Christian charitie to releive the disconsolate mindes of our people ther, and a spetiall advancement to the plantation, to tye and roote the planters myndes to Virginia by the bonds of wives and children."
>
> Virginia Company records, July 16, 1621

WIVES FOR THE SETTLERS

The members of the Virginia Company wanted to be sure the new colony would not collapse like others before it and believed that women would encourage men to work harder at making a permanent life for themselves there. Between 1619 and 1621, the Virginia Company transported about 250 young English women to Virginia. Many of the women were attracted by the Virginia Company's advertising campaign,

Right: Young women arrive in Jamestown in 1621. Few could have imagined the hardships and challenges they would have to face in the New World.

offering them a husband, a home, and a new life with a touch of adventure. Others were kidnapped from English streets and sold to planters as servants. The price for each wife was 120 pounds of tobacco to cover the cost of transportation. Many of them were married within weeks of their arrival.

SICKNESS AND FEAR

Whatever romantic notions these women may have entertained about their new lives in America, they must have been greatly tested in the first weeks and months following their arrival. The summers were hot and humid, and many colonists suffered with "Great Sweating" and "ague" (probably malaria). They lived in fear of Native American attacks, scarcely daring to venture beyond the fortified walls of their settlement into the heavily wooded land beyond. Even the clearing of forests for farmland to grow food must have seemed a daunting task. Colonists had little experience of hunting or finding edible plants. The seeds they brought with them often failed to grow. In those early, desperate years, many died from sickness and starvation.

A BRUTAL TEST

The society these women were used to back in England simply did not yet exist. The millers and cloth merchants, the craftsmen and tradespeople who together created the conditions for a civilized existence were nowhere to be found. Instead, life was a brutal test in day-to-day survival. Somehow, though, Jamestown clung on. Relations with the Native Americans gradually improved. They showed the colonists how to plant corn, which thrived in the climate.

NEW COLONIES

In 1620, a group of Separatists (Christians who wanted to separate from the Church of England) established Plymouth Colony in Massachusetts, some 496 miles north of Jamestown. Eighteen women and girls traveled with them. The Pilgrims, as these settlers were known, endured many hardships, including hunger, disease, and Native American attacks. By the spring of 1621 only four

STARVATION

"And one amongst the rest did kill his wife, powdered her, and had eaten part of her before it was known, for which he was executed, as he well deserved; now whether she was better roasted, boiled or carbonado'd [barbecued], I know not, but of such a dish as powdered wife I never heard of."

In *The Generall Historie of Virginia* (1624), the founder of Jamestown, Captain John Smith, describes a period known as the "starving time."

Right: A colonial housewife does the family's laundry—just one of dozens of domestic tasks that would have filled her day.

Above: In this busy colonial kitchen, women can be seen making bread, churning cream to make butter, spinning yarn, and warming food in the hearth.

A KIND OF SLAVERY

"For men's wives to be commanded to do service for other men, as dressing meat, washing their clothes, etc., they deemed it a kind of slavery, neither could many husbands well brook it . . ."

"The women now went willingly into the field, and took their little ones with them to set corn."

In *Of Plymouth Plantation*, written between 1620 and 1647, William Bradford, the leader of Plymouth Colony, describes in the first quote how the small number of women were initially asked to cook and clean for all the colonists and how this was resented. In the second quote, he tells how each family was given its own plot of land, and this worked much better.

of the 18 women were still alive. But, drawing strength from their faith, the Pilgrims somehow managed to survive.

As the 17th century progressed, more colonies were founded: Massachusetts Bay, New Hampshire, Connecticut, and Rhode Island joined Plymouth in New England. Maryland bordered Jamestown (which became Virginia), while New York, New Jersey, Pennsylvania, and Delaware made up the middle colonies.

DAILY TOIL
Women spent their days cooking, cleaning, doing the laundry, collecting firewood, tending the vegetable garden, dealing with domestic livestock, and caring for children. Food preparation

12

involved baking bread, churning cream to make butter, making cheese from milk and rennet, harvesting fruit and vegetables, slaughtering and butchering livestock, and brewing beer and cider. Many of the items a housewife might have bought back in England she had to make for herself, including soap and candles from animal fat, medicines from herbs, and clothing. Women made clothes from sheep's wool or from linen, which they grew from flax.

To relieve the boredom of constant labor, women would often do these chores as a group, allowing them to exchange news and gossip while they worked. They often saved themselves time and effort by trading goods and services with their neighbors or by getting their daughters to help them.

MOTHERHOOD

For women in colonial America, raising children was an almost sacred duty. In New England, well-off women usually married in their teens and immediately began raising a family. On average, they bore a child every two or three years. Families of eight or nine children were common, and some had as many as 15. Some women were still having babies when their grown daughters had started producing children of their own.

FEAR OF DYING

Childbirth, however, was a dangerous business. Between 1 and 1.5 percent of all births ended with the mother's death because of complications such as dehydration, hemorrhage, or infection. Over a lifetime, this meant a typical woman had a one in eight chance of dying in childbirth. Mothers also feared the deaths of their babies. As many as 50 percent of children died before the age of five because of disease or accident. Until the 1750s, midwives assisted women

Right: A mother nurses an infant. Colonial women spent much of their adult lives either pregnant or nursing small children.

WOMEN OF COURAGE AND CONVICTION

ANNE BRADSTREET (c. 1612–72)

Anne Bradstreet (née Dudley) was the first woman in America to have her writings published. She was born in Northampton, England, to a wealthy Puritan family. Unusually for a girl of her time, she received a good education. At 16, she married Simon Bradstreet and shortly afterward set sail with him and her parents for Massachusetts Bay Colony. The Bradstreets went on to have eight children. Alongside her duties as a housewife and mother, and despite a lifetime of poor health, Anne found time to write poetry. Her poems, strongly influenced by her Puritan faith, were simple and beautiful meditations on home, nature, love, and religion.

A MOTHER'S PLEA

"Look to my little babes, my dear remains.
And if thou love thyself, or loved'st me,
These O protect from stepdame's injury."

In her poem "Before the Birth of One of Her Children," Anne Bradstreet begs her husband to take care of her children if she dies in childbirth. Her chief fear is that they might be mistreated by a "stepdame" (stepmother).

Below: A couple mourn the death of their child. Infant mortality was all too common in colonial America. One Puritan minister lost eight of his 15 children before they were two years old.

in childbirth, but they were gradually replaced by male doctors. Female relatives and friends also lent their support.

BACK TO WORK

Most women resumed their domestic duties soon after giving birth. As the family grew, older daughters would help their mothers with infants. More affluent women employed servants to help with child care and household work. Only the wealthiest mothers could devote a lot of time to educating their children. Children were given toys and playthings, but for the most part childhood was viewed merely as a phase to be gotten through before people could assume their adult responsibilities. While boys were taught how to read and write, girls were taught merely how to be good wives and mothers.

INDENTURED SERVANTS

Many poor young English people came to the American colonies to work as indentured servants. They signed a contract called an indenture in which they agreed to work a set number of years—

usually between four and seven—for a master in the New World. In return, the master would pay for their passage across the Atlantic. About one-third of indentured servants were women, and they were primarily employed in domestic tasks. They were allowed time off on Sunday afternoons, when both male and female servants would often be seen in the local alehouse, drinking, smoking pipes, and gambling.

A HARD LIFE

Life could be tough, however. Many faced long days of exhausting labor with few breaks. Those who slacked or disobeyed were often beaten or denied food. In Chesapeake, Virginia, perhaps a quarter of all indentured servants died before their terms of labor came to an end. Some were punished by having their term extended, or their indenture might be sold to another master, so they ended up working far longer than the originally agreed term. If female servants became pregnant, the time lost to child care was added to the term of service. This was the case even if the pregnancy had been the result of rape by the master.

Below: Female cloth makers at work. In colonial America, people wove cloth from locally produced fibers such as wool, cotton, flax, and hemp.

WORK AND DRUDGERY

"What we unfortunate English People suffer here is beyond the probability of you in England to Conceive, let it suffice that I one of the unhappy Number, am toiling almost Day and Night, and very often in the Horses drudgery . . . scarce any thing but Indian Corn and Salt to eat and that even begrudged . . . almost naked no shoes nor stockings to wear . . . what rest we can get is to rap ourselves up in a Blanket and ly upon the Ground, this is the deplorable Condition your poor Betty endures. "

From a letter written in 1756 by Elizabeth Sprigs, an indentured servant in Maryland, to her father

"

MARRIAGE GIFT

"I have been thinking what would be a suitable present for me to make, and for you to receive. . . . I had almost determined on a tea table, but when I considered that the character of a good housewife was far preferable to that of being only a pretty gentlewoman, I concluded to send you a spinning wheel."

From a letter written by Benjamin Franklin to his sister Jane in 1727 to congratulate her on her marriage

Below: A wealthy 18th-century colonial couple in their opulent home. During this period the gap grew between rich and poor Americans.

One servant in Maryland, Elizabeth Greene, aborted her child to avoid having her term extended, then claimed a miscarriage. She was hanged for infanticide (the killing of her baby) in 1664.

Indentured servants could not marry until their term of service was finished, by which time they might be in their late 20s. Typically, women servants would marry former male servants. If they were fortunate, their husbands might have saved up enough to buy some land.

CHANGING TIMES

By the early 18th century, the wild landscapes that had greeted the first colonists at Jamestown and Plymouth had been replaced by cultivated fields, villages, towns, and even a few bustling cities. As the wealth of the colonies increased, homes became larger and more comfortable. For middle-class families, wooden chairs stood in the place of benches, and individual plates and cups replaced shared bowls. The colonists drank tea and flavored their food with spices. Rich Americans had many-roomed mansions filled with luxury items, such as china and silverware, upholstered furniture, and fine art. Gentlewomen spent

much of their time shopping and hosting tea parties and receptions. Like their 17th-century predecessors, they continued to wash and iron, tend their vegetable gardens, and raise chickens, but many of the goods they would once have had to make for themselves, such as clothing, candles, and soap, they could now buy. The richest women had teams of slaves to perform household tasks, allowing them to spend their time socializing, entertaining, and supervising their children's education.

THE WILD FRONTIER

While east-coast society had started to resemble that of Europe, farther to the west, on the frontier, life remained a matter of brute survival. There were few roads connecting the isolated homesteads and no schools or doctors or security from attack. Frontier families of the 1700s typically lived in log cabins with one or two rooms and wore simple, homespun clothes. The women cooked in iron pots suspended over a fire. They survived on the crops they could grow—usually wheat, oats, or rye—and any game their men brought back from the hunt. They frequently had to defend their homes from Native American attacks, and both men and women had to be handy with a musket.

WOMEN CAPTIVES

In New England, some women were taken captive by the local Native Americans and were then traded for ransom. There are also stories of European women becoming absorbed into a tribe and accepting their new existence. Mary Jemison was a frontier girl of Irish origin living in Pennsylvania. In 1755, at the age of 12, she was captured by tribespeople of the Seneca Nation. She went on to marry a Seneca man and raised a family with him. She lived happily with the tribe until her death in 1833.

WOMEN OF COURAGE AND CONVICTION

HANNAH DUSTON (1657–1736)

Hannah Duston was a colonial woman living in the frontier settlement of Haverhill, Massachusetts. In March 1697, she was captured, along with her six-day-old baby, by members of the Abenaki tribe. After witnessing them kill her baby, Hannah and two other settlers were force-marched into the wilderness. While her captors slept, she grabbed a tomahawk and attacked them. She and the other settlers killed ten Abenaki before escaping in a canoe. Hannah took the scalps of the dead Native Americans as proof of what she had done. She became a heroine in Haverhill, and a statue of her was erected in the town square.

Below: This bronze statue of Hannah Duston, made in 1879, shows her holding a tomahawk. She is believed to be the first woman in the United States to have a statue in her honor.

CHAPTER 3

WOMEN AND THE LAW

OST PEOPLE IN THE COLONIAL ERA BELIEVED THAT MEN WERE intellectually and morally superior to women. This view influenced the way women were treated under English law, which also applied to the English colonies in America.

Left: Weddings took place at the bride's house or at her church. The ceremony was usually followed by festivities and dancing.

SEXUAL INEQUALITY

A popular 17th-century pocket book titled *Advice to a Daughter*, widely read in the American colonies, stated: "There is Inequality in the Sexes, and . . . the Men, who were to be the Law-givers, had the larger share of Reason bestow'd upon them. . . . Your Sex wanteth our Reason for your Conduct, and our Strength for your Protection: Ours wanteth your Gentleness to soften, and to entertain us." The law classed women as legal incompetents, in the same category as children, criminals, and people of unsound mind. They could not vote or hold public office. In addition, their rights, such as they were, diminished when they married. An adult, single woman had a legal status known as *feme sole*, or "woman alone." She could own and sell property, make contracts, earn wages, run a business, and sue or be sued in court. All this changed, however, when she made her wedding vows.

MARRIED WOMEN

When a woman got married, she was absorbed into her husband's identity and lost all independent legal existence. As *feme covert* ("woman covered"), she could not own property, and anything she earned or inherited belonged to him. In fact, everything she possessed, even down to her clothes, became her husband's. Guardianship of any children born to a couple rested solely with the husband. In return for his wife's obedience and submission, a husband was expected to protect and provide for her.

A RESPECTFUL RELATIONSHIP

Although the law granted men seemingly unlimited power over their wives, social custom defined the boundaries of that power. A man was expected to treat his wife with respect and not rule like a tyrant. Violence against wives was deemed unacceptable in most colonies. In 1641, Massachusetts outlawed wife beating except in self-defense, and in the southern colonies, husbands were prohibited from inflicting death or permanent injury on their partners.

A SPECIAL CARE

It is also likely that a woman's personality provided a counterweight to the legal dominance of men. Wives no doubt argued with their husbands or secretly purchased things they desired. Some of the writings of the time demonstrated that, within strong marriages, mutual love and respect ensured a more equal partnership than was implied by a strict reading of the law. Massachusetts clergyman Samuel Willard (1640–1707) advised that husbands and wives should have "a special Care and Tenderness one of another."

COURTSHIP

Not only were women obliged to surrender their legal existence on their wedding day, in many cases they were not even given a choice over the groom. The law gave parents the "care and power . . . for the disposing of their children in marriage," and they usually played an active role in choosing their child's spouse. In New England, a couple could not marry without the girl's father's consent. In fact, fathers had a legal right to select which man could court his daughter, and he could sue a young man who courted his daughter without his permission.

MONEY AND PROPERTY

The parents were involved because of the economic dimension to marriage: a young man usually brought property into a marriage, and a young woman would

TURNING POINT

DAVEY V. TURNER, 1764

In 1764, the Supreme Court of the colony of Pennsylvania decided to uphold the joint deed system of conveyance. This was significant for the women of that colony because it confirmed their right to give their consent to the sale of family property. If a man wanted to sell or transfer his property, his wife would first need to give her approval to a justice of the peace. Married women had very few property rights in the colonial era, so the joint deed system, which also operated in the southern colonies, was important to them.

CHOOSING TO SERVE?

"The woman's own choice makes such a man her husband; yet being so chosen, he is her lord, and she is subject to him, yet in a way of liberty, not of bondage, and a true wife accounts her subjection her honor and freedom."

John Winthrop, Puritan leader and deputy governor of Massachusetts, 1639

"VEILED" BY MARRIAGE

"It is true, that man and wife are one person, but understand in what manner. When a small brooke or little river incorporateth with Rhodanus [the Rhone], Humber, or the Thames, the poor rivulet loseth her name. . . . A woman as soon as she is married is called covert . . . that is, "veiled"; as it were, clouded and overshadowed. . . . Her new self is her superior; her companion, her master."

A document called *The Lawes Resolutions of Womens Rights*, published in 1632 by John More, summarizes the position of married women in colonial America.

bring a dowry worth about half as much. Courtships could often only begin after letters had been exchanged by the fathers and bank accounts and family connections had been checked. A girl was not obliged to be completely passive during this process, however. If she didn't like her parents' choice, she was expected to say so since an unhappy marriage was in no one's interests. Girls from poorer families, where money was less of an issue, generally had more freedom in their choice of partner.

BROKEN MARRIAGES

Divorce was rarely granted in the southern and middle colonies, where marriage was regarded as a religious matter. Yet allowances were sometimes made. In 1744, 20 years after Susannah Cooper's husband had abandoned the marital home, she successfully petitioned the court for the right to sell his property, make contracts, and provide for herself. She remained married, however.

In New England, by contrast, marriage was a civil contract, and a court could grant a divorce if misconduct, such as adultery or wife beating, could be proved. But in a divorce, whatever the circumstances, a woman had to accept the loss of her children.

THE
LADY's LAW:
OR, A
TREATISE
OF
Feme Coverts:
CONTAINING

All the **Laws** and **Statutes** relating to WOMEN, under several HEADS:
VIZ.

I. Of Difcents of Lands to Females, Coparceners, &c.
II. Of Confummation of Marriage, ftealing of Women, Rapes, Polygamy.
III. Of the Laws of Procreation of Children ; and of Baftards or fpurious Iffue.
IV. Of the Privileges of *Feme Coverts*, and their Power with refpect to their Husband, and all others.
V. Of Husband and Wife, in what Actions they are to join.

VI. Of Eftates Tail, Jointures and Settlements, real and perfonal in Women.
VII. Of what the Wife is entitled to of the Husband's, and Things belonging to the Wife, the Husband gains Poffeffion of by Marriage.
VIII. Of Private Contracts by the Wife, Alimony, feparate Maintenance, Divorces, Elopement, &c.

THE SECOND EDITION

With divorce so rarely an option, some women simply "eloped," or fled, from disastrous marriages. Men often placed notices in newspapers warning creditors that they wouldn't honor debts incurred by their wives. One angry husband announced that his wife "hath eloped from my bed and board and refuseth to dwell with me, and therefore I take this method to warn all persons not to credit her on my account."

BEREAVEMENT

The harshness of life in the colonial period meant that marriages were most commonly terminated not by divorce or elopement, but by death. Whether a husband or wife was struck

Left: This legal treatise from 1732 contains all the English laws relating to married women, or *feme coverts*, including matters of illegitimate children, property, divorce, and elopement.

Right: An 18th-century portrait of a widow. Social pressure encouraged most widows to remarry.

down by disease, illness, accident, or exhaustion, the surviving partner usually quickly remarried. Marriage was, after all, fundamental to colonial society, where men and women had such clearly defined roles. Marrying five or six times was not uncommon. Consequently, families could be quite complex, with children from different marriages living under one roof. In fact, children in Chesapeake would refer to the woman currently married to their father as his "now wife."

WIDOWS AND INHERITANCE

In the event of a husband's death, women did find some protection under the law. Widows were provided for, partly because the state did not want to be burdened with having to support them. Under the "dower right," a widow was entitled to one-third of her late husband's land. She could not sell or bequeath this land, but she could earn money from it. On her death, the land would then pass to her husband's designated heirs. The widow might also be given guardianship of the children, although this was just as often given to a male relative or friend. A widow would usually be granted the use of the family home until her death or until their eldest son turned 21, at which stage the son would become the home owner and he would decide whether his mother could continue living there. If a widow remarried, her new husband would take over her late husband's estate, including the widow's third.

EARNING AN INCOME

There were many ways enterprising women could earn money—even if, in the case of married women, they could not legally keep it. They might sell the surplus of their vegetable gardens or seek to profit from their skills as bakers, brewers, needleworkers, dressmakers, or hatmakers. Unmarried women or widows often made a living running

THE PAIN OF SEPARATION

"I hope my Dear Mr. Byrd, will fullfill His promise when he returns to carry me to England, to visit My Dear Children. . . . But Sir, your Orders must be obeyed whatever reluctance I find thereby."

On her divorce, Elizabeth Hill Carter Byrd had to accept the loss of her children when her former husband sent them to live with his mother in England. In this letter she pleads with him to take her to England to visit them.

Above: Colonial women at work in a tinware shop. Any income earned by married women belonged to their husbands. Single women and widows, however, could keep their earnings.

A HUSBAND'S WILL

"I My Wife Alice to Have and enjoy the Land I live on for her widowhood. After her death or remarriage the Land is to return to my son Wm. Marriott."

From the will of Matthias Marriott of Surrey County, Virginia, August 18, 1722. Many men were concerned that on their wife's remarriage, their own children would be dispossessed—so they made provision for them in their will.

taverns, inns, stores, and boarding houses. There were also plenty of opportunities in the colonies for midwives and nurses. Midwives' daughters frequently followed in their mothers' footsteps. Those few women who had benefited from an education could become teachers. As a widow, Ann Wager (c. 1716–74) of Williamsburg, Virginia, supported herself as a schoolmistress for 14 years.

NEW NETHERLAND

The Dutch colony of New Netherland stood in stark contrast to the English colony in its attitude to women. Under Dutch law, which operated in Dutch colonies, women could choose from two different kinds of marriage: *manus*, in which the woman assumed the status of a minor under the guardianship of her husband, and *usus*, in which the woman retained all her rights in a partnership of equals.

Dutch law also protected women's right of inheritance, ensuring that daughters as well as sons inherited the family property and that widows received at least 50 percent of their husbands' estate. A wife could divorce her husband if he committed adultery, abandoned her, or acquired a sexually transmitted disease; she could also request half of his estate if she believed he was squandering their property.

WOMEN OF COURAGE AND CONVICTION

MARGARET REED BRENT (1601–71)

Some women deliberately avoided marrying in order to keep control of their own land and property. Margaret Brent, a wealthy Maryland landowner, was one such person. Confident and well educated, Brent conducted her affairs much as a man would, making contracts and appearing for herself in court to collect her debts. She became friends with the colony's governor, Leonard Calvert, and was even named executor of his will. Brent wanted to be the equal of men, both in business and in the political arena, and in 1648 she appeared before the Maryland Legislature and demanded the right to vote—perhaps the first woman in colonial America to do so. Not surprisingly, her request was denied. Later she moved to Virginia and bought a plantation there, which she left to her brother and his children.

Left: Margaret Brent was involved in over 100 court cases in Maryland and Virginia. She never married, despite coming under considerable pressure to do so in a society in which men outnumbered women by six to one.

TURNING POINT

NEW AMSTERDAM BECOMES NEW YORK

After the English took control of New Netherland in 1664 and renamed the capital New York, women's rights were gradually eroded. Women such as Margaret Hardenbroek were, by this time, too well established for the English takeover to affect their business—although she would have been obliged to transfer her properties and power of purchase to her husband. The new regime inhibited the next generation of women, however, and by 1691 there were just 43 women business owners in New York.

BUSINESSWOMEN

In this liberal environment, women felt encouraged to go into business for themselves. During the 1650s, there were some 134 businesswomen operating in New Amsterdam, the capital of New Netherland. The most successful of these female entrepreneurs was Margaret Hardenbroek (c. 1630–91), who arrived in New Amsterdam at the age of 22 and immediately went into business as a trader. She married a wealthy merchant, Peter de Vries, and on his death in 1661 inherited his large estate and fleet of trading ships. Hardenbroek exported furs and other goods to Holland in exchange for merchandise that she then sold in New Amsterdam. She married again and raised five children while continuing to expand her business. By her retirement in 1680, Hardenbroek was the wealthiest woman in the colony.

CHANGING ATTITUDES

By the mid-18th century, attitudes in the British colonies had begun to shift slightly, and women started to make names for themselves in the world of business. Elizabeth Timothy took over publication of the *South Carolina Gazette* on her husband's death in 1738. In Rhode Island, Mary Katherine Goddard (1738–1816), with help from her

Left: A depiction of a male and female trader in 17th-century New Amsterdam. Under Dutch law, women as well as men were encouraged to start businesses and become merchants and traders.

brother and mother, set up a printing press and published two newspapers during the 1770s. There were also signs that women were becoming more assertive in affairs of the heart. By mid-century, girls of all classes were exercising the right to refuse their parents' choice of spouse, and marriage had come to be viewed as being, to at least some degree, about love and companionship as well as an economic union.

WOMEN OF COURAGE AND CONVICTION

ELIZA LUCAS PINCKNEY (1722–93)

Eliza Lucas was born into a well-to-do British family on the Caribbean island of Antigua. When she was about 16, the family moved to Charleston, South Carolina, where her father bought several plantations. Soon afterward, her mother died and her father was recalled to Antigua, leaving Eliza in charge of the plantations. She was determined to find a cash crop that would make the plantation profitable and support the family. After failed attempts with various crops, she tried cultivating indigo. Blue indigo dye was used in Britain's growing textile industry. Eventually she found a type that thrived in the South Carolina climate. As demand for her dye expanded, Eliza gave indigo seeds to neighboring planters, and soon the dye was the colony's leading export. In 1744, she married prominent colonist Charles Pinckney, and they had four children. She resumed the running of her plantations after Pinckney's death in 1758. In 1789, Eliza became the first woman to be inducted into the South Carolina Business Hall of Fame.

Left: This sketch of laborers at work cultivating indigo was apparently drawn by Eliza Pinckney. Extracting the dye from the harvested plants was a long and painstaking process, usually carried out by slaves.

RELIGION

R ELIGIOUS POWER, LIKE POLITICAL POWER, RESTED WITH MEN IN colonial America. Nevertheless, women played a key role in the spiritual life of the colonies. They often took the lead in the religious education of their children and were, by the 1700s, the most frequent churchgoers.

THE WAY OF GOD

"I came into this Country, where I found a new World and new manners at which my heart rose [with unhappiness]. But after I was convinced it was the way of God, I submitted to it and joined to the church at Boston."

Anne Bradstreet was depressed on her arrival in Massachusetts in 1630 but describes how her faith helped her.

A REFUGE

From its earliest days, colonial America was seen as a refuge for Europeans fleeing religious persecution—a place where they could practice their Christian faith in the way they chose. The Pilgrims and Puritans led the way in the 1620s and 1630s, followed by the Quakers in 1656. Roman Catholics, Baptists, Lutherans, and Presbyterians arrived shortly afterward. The Anglican Church was also an early presence there, first in Jamestown and later spreading through the southern colonies. All Christian denominations believed that male and female souls were equal in the eyes of God, but the nature of women's role within the Church and the extent of their influence varied greatly depending on which faith they belonged to.

THE PURITANS

Puritans believed that women, like men, could receive God's grace and be members of the Church, but women nevertheless had a lower status. They entered the church by a separate door and, for most of the 1600s (until the arrival of family pews), sat apart from their male relatives. Women were barred from holding church office and were not allowed to become ministers or to

Left: This was the first church built in Boston, Massachusetts, erected in 1632. Women had no official voice in church affairs.

preach. They could not sign church covenants (declarations outlining church members' duties) or take part in the selection of ministers.

FEMALE INFLUENCE

Women did wield an informal influence in church affairs, however, particularly as the numbers of female church members grew in the early 1700s. As communities expanded, so did the distances to church for those living at their edges. Women with infants and toddlers, pregnant, or recovering from childbirth, required a church within easy walking distance. Together they would pressure their husbands to persuade the church elders to build new churches.

A FORMIDABLE FORCE

When they acted collectively, women could be a formidable force. Ministers who were popular with the female congregants tended to feel more secure in their tenure. Equally, clergymen who alienated women could find themselves vulnerable. Women acted as unofficial watchdogs of ministers' behavior both in church and the community, and a few well-placed words could destroy a reputation. Jeremiah Shepherd lost his position as minister at the church in Rowley, Massachusetts, in the

> ### GETTING TOGETHER
>
> ". . . Some women, without the knowledge of their husbands, and with the advice of some men, went to other towns, and got help, and raised the house, that we intended for a meeting house [church]."
>
> From a church history of the town of Ipswich, Massachusetts Bay Colony, 1679

Below: A depiction of the first Thanksgiving, held in Plymouth in the early fall of 1621, when 53 surviving Pilgrims gave thanks for their successful harvest.

1670s partly because the wife of the previous minister let it be known that the young man had been neglecting his studies.

A CHALLENGE TO AUTHORITY

Some Puritan women were unwilling to accept their designated role as silent, unthinking worshippers. They wanted to play a more active part in the religious life of the community. Foremost among these was Anne Hutchinson. The actions of Anne Hutchinson amounted to a direct challenge to the core beliefs of Puritan society—that it was a minister's job to interpret scripture, that this interpretation should not be questioned by non-clergy, and that women should submit to

WOMEN OF COURAGE AND CONVICTION

ANNE HUTCHINSON (1591–1643)

The daughter of a Puritan clergyman based in Alford, England, Anne Marbury was encouraged from an early age to read and discuss theology. At 21, she married William Hutchinson and had 15 children with him, of whom 13 survived. In 1634, the Hutchinsons traveled to Massachusetts Bay Colony. Here Anne set up a weekly Bible study group at her home in Boston. She was a good speaker and was soon attracting crowds of over 60 men and women. At these meetings, she often criticized the sermons of local ministers and even proposed her own interpretations of scripture. This was troubling for the colony's Puritan authorities, who disliked laypeople addressing matters of doctrine—even more so when they were women. She was tried twice, first by a civil court for challenging the government's authority and then by a church court for heresy. Found guilty on both counts, she was excommunicated from the church and banished from the colony. The Hutchinsons moved to Rhode Island in 1638 and then to a farm on Long Island, New Amsterdam, in 1643. Anne was killed there during a raid by Native Americans.

Right: Anne Hutchinson preaching in her house in Boston. Puritan leaders saw her as a threat to their male-dominated society. Today Hutchinson is remembered as the first American woman to fight for religious freedom.

PURITAN INTOLERANCE

In the wake of the Hutchinson affair, the Puritan authorities cracked down even harder on religious dissenters, including many women. In 1639, a small group of Anabaptists, led by a wealthy, educated woman named Lady Deborah Moody, arrived in Massachusetts Bay Colony. Anabaptists were Protestants who believed that only adults, not children, should receive baptism. Moody and her party were treated coldly by the colony leaders and scolded for their heretical beliefs. They did not remain there long. Two years later, in the nearby Puritan colony of New Haven, Anne Eaton, the wife of the colony's governor, was excommunicated for her Anabaptist views.

In 1645, Sarah Keayne, the sister of Anne Bradstreet, survived a shipwreck and became gripped by a religious fervor. On her return to Massachusetts Bay, she began to preach and was excommunicated in 1646 for "irregular prophesying in mixed assembly." Her husband declared she had "unwifed herself." In 1655, another woman, Joan Hogg, was convicted of "disorderly singing and idleness, and for saying she [was] commanded of Christ to do so."

MARY DYER

A more extreme Puritan response to religious dissent occurred in the case of Mary Dyer. She had been one of Anne Hutchinson's supporters, and when her heroine was excommunicated,

Above: An Anabaptist ceremony in colonial America. Anabaptists believed that people should be able to make their own professions of faith before being baptized, which is why they did not baptize infants.

 ***WOMEN OF COURAGE AND CONVICTION***

DEBORAH MOODY (c. 1612–72)

Lady Deborah Moody was born Deborah Dunch in London, England. She married a landowner, Henry Moody, and when he was knighted became Lady Deborah. After he died in 1629, Deborah became increasingly attracted to Anabaptism. Finding herself persecuted for her beliefs in England, she emigrated with her son and a group of fellow believers to New England in 1639. Their hostile reception there prompted Moody and her group to move, in 1643, to New Netherland. The Puritans were happy to see her go. The colony's deputy governor later wrote that she should not be allowed back unless she "acknowledge her ewill [evil] in opposing the churches, and leave her opinions behind her, for shee is a dangerous woeman." In 1645, the governor of New Netherland allowed Moody to establish a new settlement there (in present-day Brooklyn, New York). Moody became the first and only woman in colonial America to found her own community. She named it Gravesend, a place where people were free to worship as they chose and slavery was not allowed. She died there at age 73.

DYING WORDS

"This is to me the hour of greatest joy I ever had in this world. No ear can hear, no tongue can utter, and no heart can understand the sweet incomes and the refreshings of the spirit of the Lord, which I now feel."

The words of Mary Dyer on her way to the scaffold

Right: Mary Dyer on her way to the scaffold on June 1, 1660. Today she is honored with a statue at the State House in Boston.

Dyer had walked out of the church with her in an act of solidarity. On Hutchinson's banishment, Mary and her husband, William, followed her to Rhode Island and helped to found the new colony there. In 1657, Mary returned to Boston. By this time, she had become a Quaker, a faith the Puritans regarded as extremely heretical. Mary was imprisoned and only released after repeated pleas for mercy by her husband. A law was then passed making Quakerism a capital offense. Mary returned to Boston in 1659 to defy the anti-Quaker law and was sentenced to death, but entreaties from her son won her a last-minute reprieve. Seemingly intent on becoming a martyr, Mary returned again in 1660, and this time she was hanged.

THE QUAKERS

The Religious Society of Friends, also known as the Quakers, was a movement of Christian dissenters that began in the 1650s in England. One of them, William Penn, founded the colony of Pennsylvania as

Above: The Friends Meetinghouse in Burlington, New Jersey, built in the 1680s. Unlike in other churches at this time, Quakers allowed women to speak during prayer meetings.

a safe place for Quakers to practice their faith. The Quakers believed that women were as capable of reason and spiritual authority as men. For this reason, Quaker mothers were placed in charge of their children's religious education and were also given responsibilities in the wider community. Men and women held separate monthly meetings to oversee community affairs. While the men's meeting concerned questions of finance, trade, politics, and external relations, the women's meeting dealt with more domestic matters such as care for the poor, providing help for widows and orphans, and giving consent to marriages. Quaker mothers also acted as moral guardians of the community's female population, pronouncing on what was appropriate dress, speech, and behavior.

WOMEN TAKE THE LEAD

By the 18th century, women were going to church in greater numbers than men, in some cases forming nearly 70 percent of the congregation. They were generally considered more pious and spiritual than men, although most men regarded the study of theology as beyond a woman's capabilities.

AFRICAN AMERICANS

Many slave women gained comfort from religion. Converted to Christianity by their masters or mistresses, they identified with the Bible stories of enslaved peoples and were reassured by the New Testament

TURNING POINT

THE FIRST GREAT AWAKENING

Between the 1730s and 1770s the American colonies experienced an upsurge in religious feeling known as the First Great Awakening. Preachers such as Jonathan Edwards and George Whitefield were at the forefront of this movement, delivering powerful and theatrical sermons intended to scare people into becoming good Christians by evoking frightening images of Hell. Women seemed particularly susceptible to this message, and they flocked in their thousands to hear Edwards warn them: "The God that holds you over the pit of hell, much as one holds a spider, or some loathsome insect, over the fire, abhors you, and is dreadfully provoked."

theme of salvation through Christ. Slaves often blended their Christian worship with African religious traditions of dancing, singing, and "call and response" interactions between speaker and listeners.

NEW COMMUNITIES

By the mid-18th century, Christianity helped many slaves forge a common culture and begin to form their own communities. In northern cities such as New York and Philadelphia, slave women organized churches as centers of these emerging African-American communities. In the southern colonies, many slaves clung to their traditional African beliefs. This could cause tensions with those who had embraced Christianity, particularly where Christian notions of

Below: African Americans attend a prayer meeting. Preachers developed a passionate style that was more of a performance than a sermon. Worship frequently involved singing and dancing.

32

Above: John Wesley, founder of the Methodist movement, preaches Christianity to Native Americans in Georgia in 1736.

morality (such as its condemnation of sex outside marriage) conflicted with more tolerant African attitudes.

NATIVE AMERICANS

In contrast to European women, Native American women were figures of authority in the religious life of many tribes. Women were accorded respect in acknowledgment of their key role in many Native American myths. In the Iroquois creation story, for example, a woman falls from the Sky World and creates the Earth, and her daughter then creates good and evil.

The Seneca was a tribe within the Iroquois League. Seneca women danced to celebrate the corn crop while men chanted. In winter, Seneca women officiated at the "Thanks-to-the-Maple" ceremony, tapping the trees for the sap that would be turned into syrup. A woman would also lead the Chanters of the Dead, a priestly group that comforted men and women plagued by dreams of dead relatives.

SPIRITUAL LEADERS

The Huron of Canada elevated women to powerful roles within the tribe as sorcerers or soothsayers. The Micmac, from the same region, also accepted women as spiritual leaders. This came as quite a surprise to Catholic missionaries attempting to convert the tribes to Christianity.

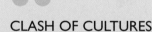

CLASH OF CULTURES

"It is a surprising fact that this ambition to act the patriarch does not only prevail among the men, but even the women meddle therewith. . . . They look upon these women as extraordinary persons, whom they believe to hold converse, to speak familiarly, and to hold communication with the sun, which they have all adored as their divinity."

Christien Le Clercq, a Roman Catholic missionary, writing about the Micmac in 1691

33

CHAPTER 5

CRIME AND PUNISHMENT

I N THE HIGHLY RELIGIOUS ENVIRONMENT OF COLONIAL AMERICA, SINS— immoral acts in the eyes of God—were regarded as crimes for which people could be tried in a court of law and, if found guilty, punished. The sins, or crimes, women were most often accused of were gossiping, infanticide, witchcraft, and sexual crimes. Sexual crimes ranged from the minor, such as kissing on the sabbath, to fornication (sex outside wedlock), adultery, and bastardy (having a child outside wedlock). Punishments, depending on the crime, included fines, pillorying, branding, whipping, burning, and hanging.

Above: In the small, highly religious communities of colonial America, women were expected to conform to the role of devoted wife and mother. Any hint of deviance was liable to be exposed by neighborly gossip and be severely punished.

RUINED WOMEN

"A licentious commerce between the sexes . . . may be carried on by men without contaminating the mind. . . . The contamination of the female mind is the necessary and inseparable consequence of an illicit intercourse with men. . . . Women are universally virtuous or utterly undone."

Lady's Magazine, August 1771

SEXUAL CRIMES

According to the Bible, Eve tempted Adam into sin by offering him a forbidden fruit. In colonial America, all women were regarded as "daughters of Eve"—morally weak and easily tempted into sinful ways. The colonists accepted that men could also be sinful, but male sin was

Right: A postcard showing two women punished by being bound together. Women in colonial times often suffered public shamings such as this for the "crimes" of nagging, scolding, arguing, or being bad tempered.

usually associated with greed and dishonesty in their business dealings, while women were more often judged by their sexual behavior. Men feared being called "knave" or "rogue," but the most damaging label for a woman was "whore." If a man indulged in a sexual sin such as adultery or fornication, it was usually assumed he had been tempted into it by a woman, or by alcohol. But a man, it was believed, could transgress sexually while remaining essentially unchanged. Not so a woman, who had to keep a tight rein on her virtue or be entirely ruined.

DOUBLE STANDARDS

These double standards were reflected in the ways that sexual crimes were dealt with by the courts. Women were convicted of sexual crimes far more often and faced harsher punishments. Between 1640 and 1685, 104 women were convicted of fornication in Essex County, Massachusetts, compared to just 35 men. Women suffered a public whipping or some form of public shaming. Men, on the other hand, were usually fined for their sexual misconduct.

CHASTITY

Why were women punished more severely for sexual crimes than men? Apart from the biblically inspired belief that women had a greater inclination toward sinfulness, there were also social and economic reasons. In this male-dominated world, where a woman was regarded as the property first of her father and then of her husband, her chastity was a highly valued asset. Once married, fidelity to her husband was as critical to his reputation as it was to hers—a cuckolded man was an object of public ridicule.

In the case of indentured servants, the crime of bastardy had an economic cost because it temporarily removed a productive female

HARSH PUNISHMENT

"I stand here for my lascivious and wanton carriages . . . "

In 1674, a young female servant was forced to wear a placard bearing these words outside the churches in Salem and Beverly, Massachusetts, or else face a whipping. Her "crimes" had included giggling at the boys' bed in the same room as hers and riding her master's horse astride.

worker from the labor market and created a child who would need financial support. Men were rarely if ever prosecuted for bastardy, mainly because paternity could not be proved.

GOSSIPS AND SCOLDS

Excluded from the formal institutions of power within their communities, colonial women often used gossip as a weapon for building and destroying reputations and policing the behavior of others. Court records show that many slander and defamation cases arose out of the deliberate spreading of rumors. But gossiping was itself regarded as a crime, and if the source was identified, she could face a turn on the ducking stool. Tied to a chair fixed to the end of a beam that hung over a river's edge, she would be ducked underwater five or six times.

Below: Scolds, shrews, and gossips were often punished by being made to wear a scold's bridle, or "the branks."

BASTARDY

"I think this law, by which I am punished, both unreasonable in itself, and particularly severe with regard to me. . . . I have brought five fine children into the world, at the risque of my life; I have maintained them well . . . without burdening the township. . . . What must poor young women do, whom customs and nature forbid to solicit the men, and who cannot force themselves upon husbands, when the laws take no care to provide them any, and yet severely punish them if they do their duty without them, . . . [to] increase and multiply; a duty from the steady performance of which nothing has been able to deter me, but for its sake I have hazarded the loss of the publick esteem, and have frequently endured publick disgrace and punishment; and therefore ought, in my humble opinion, instead of a whipping, to have a statue erected to my memory."

A speech made by a Miss Polly Baker in a Connecticut courtroom in 1747, where she was being prosecuted for the fifth time for bastardy

THE RUMOR MILL

"Brabling [gossiping] women often slander their neighbours for which their poore husbands are often brought into chargeable and vexatious suites."

Virginia Legislature, 1662

The ducking stool was also a typical punishment for women who scolded, nagged, or talked back to their husbands. Crueler still, they might be forced to wear a scold's bridle—an iron cage that covered the head, with a flat iron "curb," sometimes spiked, that projected into their mouth and pressed down on the tongue, ensuring their silence.

THE DEATH PENALTY

For serious crimes, both men and women faced the death penalty. Many women were hanged for infanticide. In the cases of Dorothy Talby (hanged 1638), Elizabeth Emmerson (1693), Esther Rodgers (1701), and Rebecca Chamblett (1733), their babies had been born outside wedlock, and their motive had almost certainly been to evade the charge of bastardy.

Some women, faced with the death penalty, "pleaded their bellies," hoping to win a reprieve by claiming they were pregnant. In such

Below: The ducking stool was a common punishment for women in colonial America. The usual victims were scolds, nags, and gossips, but ducking stools were also occasionally used on women convicted of bastardy or prostitution.

▶ **BREAKTHROUGH BIOGRAPHY**

ANNE BONNY (1697–?)

Little is known about the early life of Anne Bonny. The evidence suggests she was born in County Cork, Ireland, in 1697, the illegitimate child of an attorney, William Cormac, and his maidservant. When his adultery was made public, Cormac fled with his maidservant and daughter to Charleston, South Carolina. Stories of Anne's teenage years suggest the red-haired girl had a wild streak. She married a sailor, James Bonny, and they moved to Nassau in the Bahamas. Here she met pirate "Calico Jack" Rackham and shortly afterward left her husband to join Rackham for a life of piracy. Among the crew was another woman, Mary Read, and she and Bonny soon became good friends. In 1720, Rackham's crew was captured by a British naval vessel. Anne and Mary pleaded their bellies and were spared the death penalty. Mary later died from fever in a Jamaican prison. The fate of Anne Bonny is unknown.

Above: Anne Bonny (left) and Mary Read. According to contemporary accounts, Bonny took part in several raids, helping to capture ships and bring in treasure. She proved herself a brave fighter, winning the respect of her fellow pirates.

instances, the convicted woman would be examined by a "jury of matrons." If she was "quick with child" (in other words, if the fetus was sufficiently mature for its movements to be detected), her execution would be delayed until after the birth. Pirates Anne Bonny and Mary Read both pleaded their bellies.

WITCHCRAFT

For a woman, there were advantages to remaining unmarried in terms of independence and legal status, but there were also dangers—particularly in Puritan New England. Puritans believed that women who lacked the restraining influence of men were more likely to become possessed by the devil—more likely, in fact, to be witches.

Men and women had been accused of witchcraft in colonial America from its very beginnings. The precariousness of life in the early colonies, the outbreaks of disease, the frequently poor harvests, and sudden deaths of children and livestock encouraged colonists to seek someone to blame for their problems. Between 1620 and 1692, 114 colonists were accused of witchcraft, of whom 80 percent were women. Most of these women were widows, who lacked the protection against village gossip that a husband might have provided. Such was the case with

Anne Hibbens, a religious dissenter, who was hanged for witchcraft in 1656, two years after her husband's death.

USUAL SUSPECTS

Women accused of witchcraft tended to be assertive or argumentative types, with few friends. They were often infertile—either menopausal or childless. Goody Cole, convicted of witchcraft in New Hampshire in the 1660s, was a childless widow described as "ill-natured and ugly, artful and aggravating, malicious and revengeful." The typical suspect was also a woman with an interest in healing by means of charms, potions, and incantations. Rachel Fuller was charged with witchcraft in Hampton in 1680 after attempting to heal a sick infant, who then died.

THE SALEM WITCH TRIALS

In 1692, a collective hysteria took hold of the village of Salem, Massachusetts. It began when nine-year-old Betty Parris and her 11-year-old cousin Abigail Williams began to have fits. The girls twitched and shrieked, contorted themselves in pain, and complained of being pricked with pins.

TURNING POINT

CHANGING MASSACHUSETTS

The witch-hunting mania that swept Salem in 1692 can partly be explained by political and social changes in Massachusetts that had begun a few years earlier. In 1684, King James II of England appointed a governor to rule the colony in place of the Puritan leadership. This was followed by a large influx of immigrants to the colony's port cities and towns. Many of the newcomers were wealthy, entrepreneurial types who did not share the original colonists' strict Puritan views. This created tensions in the colony that, in Salem, manifested as an east–west split: the accusers lived in the western part of the village, home to the pious original colonists, while many of the accused lived in the east, where the richer newcomers had settled.

Left: A woman is led away by an officer of the law during the Salem witch trials of 1692. In addition to the 19 who were hanged, a further 17 people died in prison while waiting for their trials.

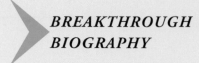

BREAKTHROUGH BIOGRAPHY

SARAH GOOD (1655–92)

One of the first to be accused and convicted of witchcraft in Salem was Sarah Good. She was a poor woman, an outsider in the village, who went door to door begging for charity. Many of those who turned her away blamed her for the subsequent deaths of their livestock. When she entered the courtroom for her trial, her accusers immediately fell into fits. One girl alleged Good had attacked her with a knife. Others claimed to have seen her flying on a broomstick. Even her husband and four-year-old daughter testified against her. Sarah Good always denied she was a witch. She was hanged on July 16, 1692.

A WITCH'S TRIAL

"The worshipful Mr. Hathorne asked [Martha Corey] why she afflicted those children. She said she did not afflict them. He asked her, "Who did then?" She said, "I do not know; how should I know?" The . . . afflicted persons . . . did vehemently accuse her in the assembly of afflicting them, by biting, pinching, strangling, etc.; and that they did in their fit see her likeness coming to them, and bringing a book to them. She said she had no book. They affirmed she had a yellow bird that used to suck betwixt her fingers; and being asked about it, if she had any familiar spirit that attended her, she said she had no familiarity with any such thing . . . "

Deodat Lawson, a visiting minister, describes the trial of Martha Corey

Soon other girls also began to have seizures. When questioned, the girls named three local women who, they claimed, had appeared as spirits in their nightmares. The accused women were seen as outcasts in the village because of their poverty, unseemly behavior, or—in the case of a slave named Tituba—ethnicity.

A POWERFUL NETWORK

Over the next few months, more and more accusations were made as the girls, egged on by community leaders, named more names, including those of wealthy and prominent citizens. Soon it seemed that the entire village was threatened by a powerful network of men and women in league with the devil. And those few who dared voice their disbelief about the affair were often then accused themselves.

Before the Salem witch trials, the usual official response to accusations of witchcraft in New England had been to let the villagers resolve it themselves. This time, though, the judicial authorities not only stepped in, but appeared actively to encourage the witch hunt. The trials began in May 1692, and by the end of July, 19 people had been hanged, 14 of them women. Over a hundred others—many of them of high social standing—were put in cells awaiting trial.

APPEALS FOR MERCY

Eventually, when events appeared to be spinning out of control, a group of wealthy merchants privately appealed to the non-Puritan royal governor, William Phips, to intervene. In October, Phips banned any further arrests and dismissed the court. By January 1693, all the remaining prisoners had been acquitted. The witch hunt was over.

RESTRICTIVE LIVES

In later years, several of the accusers admitted they had lied, or been deluded by Satan, and expressed repentance for what they had done. So what motivated these girls in the first place? No one can answer this for sure, but a clue may lie in the nature of their everyday existence. Puritan children had few toys and games, and young girls led especially restrictive lives, performing household tasks and preparing for marriage. They no doubt greatly enjoyed the sudden attention and power of their new status as witch hunters.

Above: An illustration of one of the witch trials at Salem. In this superstitious age, allegations that seem laughable today were taken seriously by the court. Defendants were examined for "devil's birthmarks" or webbed hands, and witnesses claimed they had seen witches flying on broomsticks and appearing before them as ghosts.

Left: Bridget Bishop was the first victim of the Salem witch trials. She had been married three times, entertained guests in her home until late, enjoyed drinking, and dressed colorfully—behavior that was bound to arouse suspicion in Puritan society. She was hanged on June 10, 1692.

41

CHAPTER 6

AFRICAN AMERICANS

THE BLACK POPULATION OF THE AMERICAN COLONIES WAS VERY small to begin with. In 1623, there were just 23 Africans in Virginia. By 1650, this number had risen to 300, about 3 percent of the population. Black people arrived as indentured servants, but once their term of indenture was served, they were free to earn money, buy and sell property, appear in court, hire white or black laborers, and marry.

TURNING POINT

LAWS

- Massachusetts, 1641: Slavery is legalized.

- Virginia, 1662: All children born to a slave mother are to be enslaved: slavery becomes hereditary.

- Virginia, 1664: Children from interracial marriages are to be enslaved.

- Virginia, 1667: Baptism into the Christian faith is closed off as a route to freedom for slaves.

- Virginia and Maryland, 1672: Black planters are forbidden to purchase the labor of white servants.

- Virginia, 1682: All servants arriving in the colony whose parents and native countries were not Christian are deemed to be slaves.

- Virginia and Maryland, 1691: Interracial marriage is banned.

Above This Boston notice from about 1700 advertises a "choice cargo of about 250 fine healthy negroes, just arrived." By this time, the slave trade was at its height. Shortly after arrival, African men and women would be sold at auction like cattle.

THE RISE OF SLAVERY

There was little obvious racism in early colonial politics and society. African men and women were brought to the colonies as indentured servants on fixed-term contracts. The evidence suggests they were treated courteously by their neighbors and fairly under the law. By mid-century, conditions had started to change. English servants began to demand better working conditions, including breaks during the heat of the day and days of rest. They asserted these rights as free-born English citizens. But when African servants tried to claim similar rights, the local courts refused to acknowledge them. Wealthy colonists, especially southern planters, started to see the advantages of enslaving the black population. In addition to lacking English citizens' customary rights, Africans were also much more resilient to the summer heat and hot-weather diseases such as malaria.

RESTRICTING FREEDOMS

Gradually laws were introduced across the colonies to prevent Africans from escaping a life of servitude, while other laws restricted their social and economic freedoms. The legal framework supporting the institution of slavery began to take shape. In 1698, the English parliament ruled that any British subject could traffick in slaves, and this marked the beginning of a huge expansion in the slave trade. By 1774, nearly 450,000 blacks were living in the American colonies, almost 90 percent of them in the South.

JOURNEY AND ARRIVAL

For Africans captured by slave traders, the ordeal would begin with a forced march in chains from their home village in West Africa to the Atlantic coast. They were then branded and made to endure the horrors of the Atlantic crossing, known as the "middle passage." Chained in rows in filthy, stifling conditions, nearly one-fifth died on each voyage.

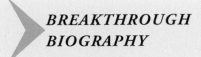

BREAKTHROUGH BIOGRAPHY

ELIZABETH KEY
(1630–after 1665)

Born in Warwick County, Virginia, Elizabeth Key was the illegitimate daughter of Thomas Key, a white planter, and his black slave. Before his death in 1636, Key entrusted Elizabeth's guardianship to a friend, Humphrey Higginson, and stipulated that Elizabeth should be given her freedom when she turned 15. Higginson then sold her to another planter, John Mottram, who failed to free her at the appointed time. When Mottram died in 1655, Elizabeth sued his estate for her freedom. Although the Mottram estate had classified her as a "negro," Elizabeth argued that as the child of a free man and a baptized Christian, she should also be free. After a long struggle, Elizabeth finally won her freedom in 1656—the first woman of African ancestry to achieve this in colonial America. In response, the Virginia legislature passed a law in 1662 to the effect that all children born in the colony would follow the status of the mother—closing off this potential route to freedom.

Below: A Dutch slave ship arrives at Jamestown, Virginia, in 1619. Unlike Elizabeth Key, the vast majority of African men and women shipped to the American colonies faced a sad and brutal existence as slaves, with no chance of winning their freedom.

BIRTH ON BOARD SHIP

"I saw pregnant women give birth to babies while chained to corpses which our drunken overseers had not removed. . . . Packed spoon-fashion they often gave birth to children in the scalding perspiration from the human cargo. . . . On board the ship was a young negro woman chained to the deck, who had lost her senses soon after she was purchased and taken on board."

Part of an eyewitness account of the middle passage by a slave trader

Slaves arrived weakened and often sickly from their ordeal but quickly had to adjust to an alien culture and climate, learn new skills, and master a foreign tongue.

WORKING LIFE

During the 17th century, slave women in Virginia, Maryland, and North Carolina—the so-called Upper South—were sent to labor in the fields alongside the men in work gangs of two to 12 laborers. They worked six days a week, often until long past sunset. Daytime work included planting, tending, and harvesting tobacco and corn—all done by hand. In the evenings, they stripped the tobacco leaves from their stems or shelled corn.

Below: Africans endured terrible conditions aboard the slave ships that took them to the Americas. Between the 16th and 19th centuries, an estimated two million died on these voyages as a result of disease, beatings, suicide, or starvation.

EARLY DEATH

In the rice-growing regions of South Carolina and Georgia, known as the Lower South, slave women also worked in the fields. Here, though, instead of working in gangs, each slave was given a task that he or she had to complete by the end of the day. The hardest of these tasks—pounding the grain with mortar and pestle—was given to women. Mortality rates among slaves were higher in the Lower South than elsewhere in the colonies because of the prevalence of disease in this region. The highest mortality rates of all were suffered by the women who pounded the grain.

In the middle and northern colonies, slaves were far fewer in number and most commonly found in the cities. The men were employed in workshops or on the docks, while the women were mostly in domestic service—cooking, cleaning, washing, gardening, and looking after the master's children.

DIVISION OF LABOR

By the mid-18th century, agricultural advances in the Upper South had changed the working lives of slave women on the larger plantations. The move from hoe to plow farming enabled planters to expand their activities to include wheat and rye cultivation, fishing, milling, and timber production. Farm work was divided along gender lines: male slaves did heavy or skilled work such as plowing, wood chopping, carpentry, and blacksmithing, while women did lighter, unskilled work such as hoeing, weeding, cleaning stables, and spreading manure. Domestic work in the planter's household was given to young girls or older women incapable of working in the fields.

FAMILY LIFE

Until the emergence of a large American-born black population in the 18th century, the ratio of African men to women in the colonies was heavily skewed in favor of males, remaining about two to one until the early 1700s. This made it hard for men and women to form relationships and start families. Those who did often belonged to

A SUGAR PLANTATION.

Above: African slaves at work on a sugar plantation in the Deep South. Sugar plantations were labor intensive. Slaves planted, fertilized, weeded, harvested, stripped, and cut the cane before sending it to the mill. Here more slaves crushed the cane and boiled the juice to produce sugar and molasses.

OWNERSHIP

"In case you have not only male but likewise female Negroes, they must intermarry, and then the children are all your slaves. But if you possess a male Negro only, and he has an inclination to marry a female belonging to a different master . . . it is no advantage to you, for the children belong to the master of the female. It is therefore advantageous to have Negro women."

An observation by Swedish naturalist Pehr Kalm in *Travels into North America (1753–1761)*, published in 1773

Right: A reconstruction of typical slave quarters in Williamsburg, Virginia. There was often a piece of land next to slave quarters where slaves were allowed to grow their own food.

different masters and could not live or raise their children together. African women bore an average of just three children, of which only two were likely to survive. As a result, there was no natural increase in the slave population until well into the 18th century.

LIVING TOGETHER

The expansion of the plantations in the Upper South in the mid-18th century meant that for the first time, large numbers of slaves lived and worked together. In this environment, stable families became possible. Slaves could not legally marry, but many pledged their love to each other. Slave women typically had their first child at 19 and produced an average of eight children over their lives, giving birth about once every 27 to 29 months. Frequent pregnancy benefited mothers since they could expect more food and fewer working hours. Fertile mothers were also less likely to be sold away from friends and family.

CHILD REARING

On the larger plantations, children typically lived with both parents until the age of ten, usually in a two-family log cabin. An emerging network of friends and relatives would help mothers with child rearing. On smaller plantations, the slaves usually lived altogether in one large cabin, making privacy for couples difficult. If couples lived on separate plantations, the children would live with the mother. Fathers would make nightly and Sunday journeys to visit their families if they were sufficiently close and their master permitted it.

AN UNHAPPY CONDITION

Conditions in the Lower South worked against slave families. The vast majority of rice plantations in Georgia, for example, had fewer than 50 slaves, and 13 percent had just one. In addition, men greatly outnumbered women, and some plantations were virtually single sex. Georgia planters showed little interest in creating new slave generations through natural increase, preferring to import them, and most forbade relationships between slaves on different plantations. Consequently, only a little over a quarter of slave women formed relationships and lived with their partners. Just over half of these couples had a child living with them—the rest had none.

Slave families were even rarer in the northern colonies, where urban households often consisted of just one slave. Some masters would sooner sell a pregnant slave than be burdened with the costs of child care.

BROKEN FAMILIES

Slave families did not often remain together long. Between the ages of ten and 14, children were usually sold, perhaps

BREAKTHROUGH BIOGRAPHY

PHILLIS WHEATLEY (c. 1753–84)

Born in West Africa, Phillis Wheatley was snatched from her home and taken to America at the age of eight. She was bought by a wealthy Boston tailor, John Wheatley. He and his wife, Susanna, gave Phillis a good education, and the young girl soon displayed a remarkable gift for words. With the Wheatleys' encouragement, Phillis began writing poems for public occasions, and she became famous throughout Boston. On a trip to London in 1773, a collection of her poetry was published, making her the first female African American published writer. Her master died in 1778, and Phillis became free. She married a free black man, John Peters. However, her later life proved unhappy. Two of their children died, and her husband was imprisoned for debt. Poverty forced Phillis into service as a scullery maid. She died alone at age 31, followed hours later by her sickly infant daughter.

Below: Phillis Wheatley's literary talents challenged a major justification for the slave trade—the European assumption of African inferiority.

47

RUNNING AWAY

"[Hagar is probably hidden] in some Negro Quarter [cabin] as her father and mother Encourage her Elopements."

A runaway notice placed in the *Maryland Gazette* announces the probable location of 14-year-old slave girl Hagar, who kept running away from the man she'd been sold to, returning each time to her parents.

Below: A reconstruction of the interior of a typical slave cabin. Slaves lived in cramped conditions, often with two families sharing a single two-room dwelling. The cabins usually had thin walls and dirt floors.

never to see their parents again. Deaths and marriages in the master's family also often preceded a heartbreaking separation in a slave family, as slaves were either sold or sent to separate households.

THE RISE OF SLAVE COMMUNITIES

The natural growth of the slave population led to a shift of the population from African to African-American, so that by 1774 just 20 percent of American slaves were African born. By the 1750s, a distinctive African American community had begun to develop across the South. Its members shared a common tongue—English—and most shared a common faith in Christianity. In the Upper South, they lived together in slave cabins, away from the master's family, giving them space to organize themselves and establish their own customs, including naming and burial rituals.

WOMEN TRADERS

Many slave quarters were surrounded by land on which the slaves could grow their own food. An internal market soon arose in which slaves traded surplus crops and livestock, game, fish, and goods stolen from the master's stores. Slave women played an important role in the

internal market, producing and selling baked goods, garden vegetables, and handcrafted objects. In the Lower South, slaves grew traditional African crops, including tania and peppers as well as rice and corn. In South Carolina, the women took charge of selling the produce on market days at Charleston, and these female traders became known for their sharp business sense when negotiating prices with customers.

The evidence suggests that the slave women market traders of Charleston, South Carolina, were not too popular with their white customers. In 1763, they were being labeled "insolent," "abusive," "notorious," and "impudent." Five years later, the city's grand jury complained of the "many idle negro wenches, selling dry goods, cakes, rice, etc. in the markets."

HORRID MASSACRE IN VIRGINIA.

The Scenes which the above Plate is designed to represent are—Fig 1. a Mother intreating for the lives of her children.—2. Mr. Travis, cruelly murdered by his own Slaves.—3. Mr. Barrow, who bravely defended himself until his wife escaped.—4. A comp. of mounted Dragoons in pursuit of the Blacks.

Above: The slave revolts of the 18th century inspired other, more violent ones in the 19th century. This picture shows an uprising in Southampton County, Virginia, in 1831, in which 55 white people were killed.

PUNISHMENT AND REBELLION

These communities developed despite the exhausting labor and often brutal conditions that were the daily reality of a slave's life. If slaves were deemed not to be working hard enough or to be talking too much or using their native language, or if they were suspected of stealing or trying to run away, the punishments could be harsh for both men and women. They included being shackled, whipped, forced to walk a treadmill, or even death by hanging. Women also faced the additional threat of being forced into sexual relationships to satisfy the master's lust or for purposes of reproduction.

In such circumstances, slaves sometimes rebelled. Women occasionally tried to poison their masters or burn down their homes. They were, however, less likely to run away than men, being reluctant to abandon their children and elderly dependents. Yet slave women did take part in the rare organized slave rebellions, including uprisings in New York City in 1712 and 1741, and the Stono River rebellion in South Carolina in 1739.

TURNING POINT

NEW YORK SLAVE REVOLT OF 1712

On April 6, 1712, 23 black slaves set fire to a building on Maiden Lane in New York City in one of the earliest slave uprisings in British America. While white colonists tried to put out the fire, the slaves attacked them, then ran off. Nine whites died and six were injured in the uprising. The authorities arrested 70 blacks, including several women. Twenty-one were executed. The revolt led to more restrictive laws governing the lives of slaves.

CHAPTER 7
NATIVE AMERICANS

BY THE 1500S, NATIVE AMERICAN MEN AND WOMEN HAD DEVELOPED clearly defined roles within each village and tribe: the men hunted, waged war, traded, and negotiated with other tribes; the women, meanwhile, tended the crops, raised the children, and took care of the domestic sphere.

FEMALE POWER

With men absent from home for much of the time, women wielded a great deal of authority within the village. In fact, many tribes were matrilineal—people traced their lineage, or ancestry, through their mother's family. In such societies, when a man married, he moved into his wife's family home, and if the couple later divorced, it was the man who had to leave.

Below: Blackfoot Indian women put up tepees as they establish a new camp. The Blackfoot were a hunting people of the northwestern Great Plains. They broke camp at regular intervals to follow the buffalo herds.

THE FOOD SUPPLY

Since women were responsible for agriculture, they controlled the community's food supplies. They stored any surplus in pots underground to which they alone had access. This could be a great source of leverage: if they disapproved of a proposed war, for example, they could simply refuse to supply grain and dried meat to the men.

LAWS OF THE IROQUOIS

The Iroquois was a confederacy of five nations based in the northeast of what became the United States. Men held formal political power in these tribes, but channels were available through which women could express their views. For example, women could address the Council of Elders, the highest ruling body of the Iroquois, through a male intermediary. The most powerful women among the Iroquois were the elderly heads of each household. They chose which men could be candidates for chief, and they could also bring about the removal of a chief who failed to meet their approval.

WORK

Women's lives were centered on their village and home. They planted and harvested the corn, beans, and squash, which they supplemented with wild fruits. They fetched water and gathered fuel for fires. Everything they needed, including farming tools, cooking utensils, baskets, bags, sacks, and pots, they made themselves from natural materials such as leather, bone, shell, clay, and bark.

SEWING, PRESERVING, AND BUILDING

Women made clothes from animal hides sewn with bone needles and deer sinews. They decorated the clothes with shells, beads, dyed porcupine quills, and paint. To get their families through the winter, women preserved food such as corn, pumpkin, fish, and meat by drying and then burying it in

WOMEN OF COURAGE AND CONVICTION

WEETAMOO
(c. 1635–76)

While most Native American women exercised their power within the domestic sphere, a few of royal blood became political leaders. One of the most famous was Weetamoo, wife of Wamsutta, the chief of the Wampanoag tribe. For most of her life, a peace treaty existed between the Wampanoag and the neighboring colony of Plymouth. However, during a land dispute in 1664, Plymouth officials seized Wamsutta, and he died mysteriously during interrogation. Weetamoo suspected the English had killed her husband. Her brother-in-law Metacomet was the new tribal chief, and Weetamoo also held a position of authority in the tribe, with 300 warriors under her command. In June 1675, Metacomet and Weetamoo led their people in an attack on the English. They raided Lancaster and a few other towns but were soon defeated. Most of their followers were killed or sold into slavery. Weetamoo herself drowned in a river while trying to escape.

Below: Metacomet leads a raid on an English settlement in 1675. The colonists knew Metacomet as "King Philip," and named his and Weetamoo's rebellion King Philip's War.

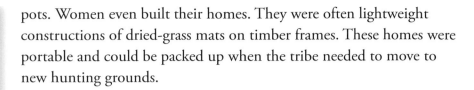

WOMEN'S PURSUITS

"They have the care of the cooking and the household, of sowing and gathering corn, grinding flour, preparing hemp and tree-bark, and providing the necessary wood. And because there still remains plenty of time to waste, they employ it in gaming, going to dances and feasts, chatting and killing time, and doing just what they like with their leisure."

French missionary Gabriel Sagard, *The Long Journey to the Country of the Hurons* (1632)

pots. Women even built their homes. They were often lightweight constructions of dried-grass mats on timber frames. These homes were portable and could be packed up when the tribe needed to move to new hunting grounds.

FARMING

Women headed into the fields early, just after dawn, carrying their small children in cradle boards on their backs. While the younger women dug and hoed, the older ones scared away the birds and other animals. Although they worked hard, women set their own pace and often shared jobs, usually leaving themselves time at the end of the day for enjoyment.

CHILDHOOD AND PUBERTY

Mothers showed their daughters how to plant corn, pound it into meal, bake bread, and perform all the other tasks they would need to do in adulthood. Girls, like boys, were taught early in life to tolerate hardship and discomfort. Mothers drenched them with cold water or snow and let them play outside without clothes. Yet children were rarely verbally or physically punished. According to Jesuit missionary Pierre de Charlevoix, if a mother was truly provoked, she might weep and declare a child had dishonored her. The worst punishment he witnessed was a mother flicking water in her child's face.

Among east coast tribes, the onset of puberty was a significant moment in a girl's life. Menstruation was viewed as a sign of heightened power in a woman, which could, according to some tribes, bring bad luck. Girls were isolated for the duration of their first period. On their return, they were washed, dressed in new clothes, and permitted to re-enter the family home.

COURTSHIP

When a man wanted to marry, he would first ask the permission of the girl's parents. This would usually be done through an intermediary, such as a brother or

Left: A mother carries her baby on a cradle board. Cradle boards kept infants secure and comfortable while freeing mothers to move around and work.

uncle. Young men of the Huron painted their faces to improve their physical appeal; they also sent their loved one gifts of jewelry. Parents often demanded that their prospective son-in-law prove himself as a hunter and warrior before they would agree to a match. Marriages created ties between different clans, and often senior clan members had to be consulted before a match could be approved.

MARRIAGE

Weddings were celebrated with feasts for family, friends, and in some cases the whole community. In many tribes, both families would exchange gifts. In others, the husband

Below: This painting shows the capture of Pocahontas by English colonists in 1612. Sadly, the peace she helped bring about did not last long. Within a few decades of Pocahontas's death, the English had driven the Powhatan from their lands.

WOMEN OF COURAGE AND CONVICTION

POCAHONTAS (c. 1595–1617)

The daughter of Chief Powhatan of the Powhatan Confederacy, Pocahontas was about 12 years old when the English settled Jamestown. "Pocahontas" was her nickname, meaning "naughty one"—her real name was Matoaka. Colony leader John Smith later claimed that the young princess had saved him from being executed by her father, but this is probably untrue. What is certain is that the initially cordial relations between the colonists and the Powhatan soon deteriorated, and in 1612 the English took Pocahontas prisoner. During her captivity, she married 28-year-old colonist John Rolfe and converted to Christianity, taking the name Rebecca Rolfe. The marriage helped to make peace between the colonists and Powhatan's people. The couple later had a son, Thomas. In 1616, Rolfe took Pocahontas to England, where she was introduced to London society and met the king. Just before their return to Virginia, she became ill and died.

Above: A 1590 engraving of a Native American husband and wife preparing a meal together. Native American marriages were easy enough to end, yet many unions endured, perhaps because the primary motivation for them was love.

would pay a "bride price" to his wife's family. Among matrilineal peoples, such as the Iroquois, the husband joined his bride's clan and went to live in her family home.

DIVORCE

Divorce was usually a simple procedure, with either partner free to walk away from an unhappy marriage. One European missionary was shocked to hear a Miami Native American explain that he and his neighbor had agreed to swap wives. Couples were not bound by the laws of property and inheritance or the Christian beliefs that made divorce so rare and difficult for the colonists.

The ease of divorce did not mean that marriages were entered into lightly. Families tried to ensure that couples were compatible in the hope that their union would last. In most tribes, couples were allowed to share a bed before the wedding for this reason. The Micmac

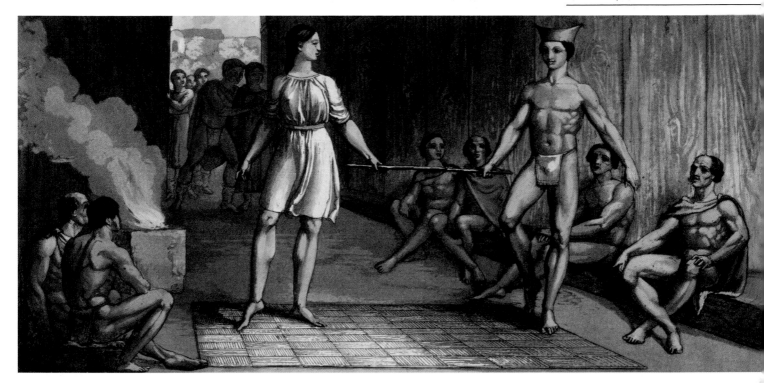

Above: Wedding traditions varied from tribe to tribe, but most included dancing and feasting. Gifts of clothing and food were often exchanged between the two families. In some tribes, the couple would symbolize their union by drinking from a wedding vase. In others, they would smoke from the same pipe.

encouraged couples to abstain from sex for a year after marrying to ensure their relationship was about more than sexual attraction.

ADULTERY

A common reason for divorce was adultery. Among the Ottawa, a man had to prove his wife's infidelity before he could divorce her. An Illinois husband could disfigure or even kill his wife if she was unfaithful. Whatever the cause of divorce, the couple's children would always remain with the mother or her clan.

PREGNANCY AND CHILDBIRTH

As with menstruation, a woman's spiritual power was believed to increase during pregnancy and childbirth. This power was feared by most tribes for the bad luck it might bring. When a woman went into labor, she retired to a specially prepared hut in the woods, beyond the perimeter of the village. Sometimes she delivered the baby alone and

BREAKTHROUGH BIOGRAPHY

MARY MUSGROVE (c. 1700–after 1763)

Coosaponakesee was the daughter of an English trader from South Carolina and a Creek Native American woman. She began her life among her mother's people. In this matrilineal tribe, children took the clan identity of their mothers, so Coosaponakesee was accepted, despite her mixed heritage. In 1710, her mother died and the girl was sent to live among the English. She was rechristened Mary and educated as a Christian. In 1716, Mary married a trader, John Musgrove. For the Creeks, marriage traditionally created kinship ties between different tribes. For Mary, it created a bridge between the Creeks and the whites. She helped her husband negotiate with the Creek Nation and set up a profitable trading post in the new territory of Georgia. In 1733, when the colony of Georgia was established, Mary was again employed as an intermediary between the English and the local Creek Native Americans. Eight years later, she persuaded the Creeks to support the British in their conflict with the Spanish. She married twice more and retired to St. Catherine's Island in 1760, where she died.

sometimes with the help of a midwife or female relative. Several male European observers were amazed at how rarely Native American women cried out in pain during labor. Some even believed they were built differently from European females. In fact, these women saw childbirth in the way a male warrior would view a battle—an opportunity to show their bravery. Micmac women sometimes even asked to have their mouths stopped up to ensure they remained quiet.

EARLY CHILDHOOD

In most Native American tribes, mothers would breastfeed their children until they were five or six. Soon after a woman gave birth, she would resume her domestic tasks. She would carry her swaddled infant in a cradle board on her back, freeing her hands for work. Mothers would decorate the cradle boards with paint, beads, feathers, and porcupine quills. They would similarly adorn their child's clothing. By using a cradle board, a mother could remain almost constantly with her child during the early years.

Below: A Native American couple with their young child. While boys were taught hunting, fighting, and weapon-making skills, girls were instructed in how to make clothes, prepare meals, and other household duties.

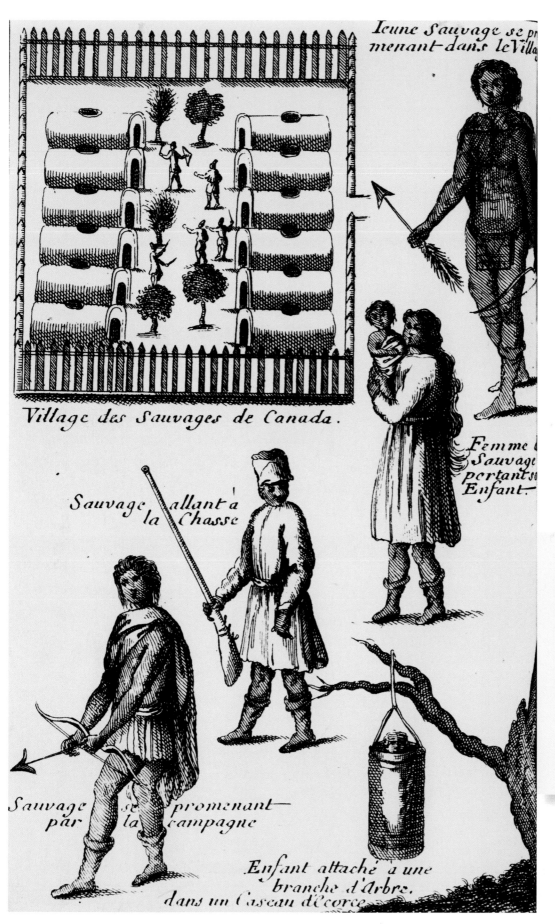

Village des Sauvages de Canada.

Icune Sauvage se pr
menant dans le Villag

Femme
Sauvage
portant se
Enfant.

Sauvage allant à
la Chasse

Sauvage se promenant
par la campagne

Enfant attaché à une
branche d'Arbre
dans un Caseau d'écorce

Left: These sketches were made by Louis Armand, Baron of Lahontan, a French soldier and explorer who spent time among Native American tribes in Canada, Wisconsin, and Minnesota in the late 1600s. They show a village, some hunters, a mother and child, and an infant hanging in an early type of baby carrier from the branch of a tree.

CHAPTER 8

THE PERIOD IN BRIEF

THE ROLE OF WOMEN IN EARLY AND COLONIAL AMERICA WAS, FOR the most part, confined to the domestic sphere. The period did not see any major advance in women's status, but a few brave, pioneering souls emerged who would inspire the generations that followed.

EUROPEAN WOMEN

Among the European colonists, the dominant creeds of Puritanism and Anglicanism dictated that women were seen as naturally inferior to men. This view was reflected in the laws of the period, which gave women little or no opportunity for a public voice in community affairs and made them financially dependent on their fathers or husbands. Their lives were almost entirely made up of domestic work and child rearing. A few remarkable women managed to overcome the severe restrictions placed on their sex and make a mark on society, including Ann Bradstreet, Margaret Reed Brent, Eliza Lucas Pinckney, and Ann Smith Franklin.

AFRICAN-AMERICAN WOMEN

If the life of a European colonial woman was hard, it was many times more so for African-American slave women. Torn from their homes and brought under terrible conditions to a life of servitude in an alien land, these women had no common culture to give them comfort in their suffering. They were forced

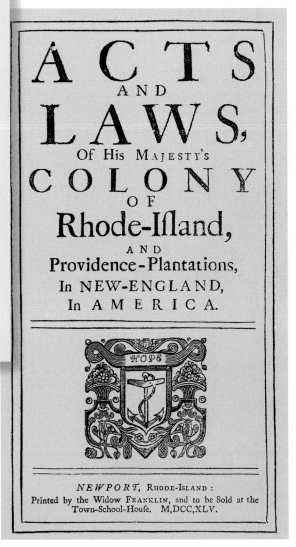

ACTS AND LAWS, Of His MAJESTY's COLONY OF Rhode-Island, AND Providence-Plantations, In NEW-ENGLAND, In AMERICA.

HOPE

NEWPORT, RHODE-ISLAND:
Printed by the Widow FRANKLIN, and to be Sold at the Town-School-House. M,DCC,XLV.

Right: The frontispiece of a book published by Ann Smith Franklin, America's first female newspaper editor.

to work long hours under the hot sun and were given virtually no opportunities to form stable relationships or establish communities. Gradually slave communities emerged in the 18th century and with them the beginnings of an African-American culture. In the North, where conditions were less harsh, a young black woman named Phillis Wheatley wrote poetry that charmed rich white society, but even she was to die in poverty and obscurity.

NATIVE AMERICAN WOMEN

Native American women generally had far more freedom and power than European or black women. Although their role was also mainly centered on the home, the long periods of male absence enabled them to gain an influential status within their family and community. The lack of a religious moral code also made them much freer than colonial women in matters of sex, marriage, and divorce.

Together European, African-American, and Native American women played a key role in the transformation of the New World during the 17th and 18th centuries. They may not have held much formal power, but through their labor and sacrifices, they helped shape the early history of America.

A FOCUS ON WOMEN

"Remember the ladies, and be more generous and favorable to them than your ancestors. Do not put such unlimited power into the hands of the Husbands. Remember all Men would be tyrants if they could. If particular care and attention is not paid to the Ladies we are determined to foment a Rebellion, and will not hold ourselves bound by any Laws in which we have no voice, or Representation."

Abigail Adams, in a letter to her husband, John Adams, a founding father of the United States, March 1776

Below: An American family on the eve of the Revolution. In the century to come, women would no longer be content to play a purely domestic role.

TIMELINE

1492	Christopher Columbus becomes the first European to make landfall in America since Leif Eriksson in c. 1000.
1591	Walter Raleigh's Roanoake colony fails.
1587	Virginia Dare is the first English child to be born in the New World.
1607	Jamestown, Virginia, is the first successful English colony to be founded in North America.
1608	The first women arrive at Jamestown.
1608	Samuel de Champlain founds Québec.
1612–17	Pocahontas is taken prisoner, marries John Rolfe, converts to Christianity, travels to England, and dies.
1619	The first Africans arrive in Jamestown; women start to arrive in large numbers from this date.
1620	The Pilgrims found Plymouth Colony in Massachusetts. Women and girls travel there with their husbands and fathers.
1624	The Dutch colony of New Netherland is founded.
1630	Anne Bradstreet arrives in Massachusetts.
1633	Maryland is founded.
1636	Rhode Island and Connecticut are founded.
1638	Delaware and New Hampshire are founded. Anne Hutchinson is excommunicated and banished from Massachusetts Bay Colony.
1640s–90s	Legislation is passed throughout the colonies restricting the freedoms of Africans, and legitimizing slavery.
1645	Lady Deborah Moody founds Gravesend in present-day Brooklyn, New York.
1648	Margaret Reed Brent appears before the Maryland Legislature and demands the right to vote.
1650s	English colonists drive the Powhatan Confederacy out of Virginia.
1656	Elizabeth Key becomes the first woman of African ancestry in colonial America to win her freedom.
c.1652	Margaret Hardenbroek arrives in New Amsterdam and embarks on her career as a trader.
1653	North Carolina is founded.
1660	Quaker martyr Mary Dyer is hanged in Boston for heresy.
1663	South Carolina is founded.
1664	New Jersey is founded. Britain annexes the Dutch colony of New Netherland.
1671	English explorers are the first Europeans to cross the Appalachians.
1675	Weetamoo and Metacomet lead their people in an attack on the English colonists of Plymouth, Massachusetts.
1682	Pennsylvania is founded.
1689–97	King William's War: the English and their Iroquois allies fight the French and their Huron allies in Canada and New England.

1692	The Salem witch trials result in the hanging of 19 innocent people, 14 of them women.
1697	Hannah Duston is captured by Abenaki Indians. She kills ten of them before making her escape.
1698	The British parliament legalizes the trafficking of slaves, sparking a huge expansion of the slave trade.
1702–13	Queen Anne's War: Britain and the Netherlands fight France and Spain. Britain acquires Newfoundland, Acadia, and Hudson Bay.
1710s	English colonists drive the Tuscarora and Yamasee out of the Carolinas.
1712	The New York Slave Revolt.
1720	Pirates Anne Bonny and Mary Read "plead their bellies" to avoid being hanged.
1730s–70s	The religious revivalist movement, the First Great Awakening, sweeps the American colonies.
1730–55	English colonists drive the Shawnee and Delaware west down the Ohio River.
1733	Georgia is founded, with help from Mary Musgrove.
1735	Ann Smith Franklin takes over the running of her late husband's newspaper.
1739	Eliza Lucas Pinckney begins to experiment with indigo cultivation.
1744–48	King George's War between Britain and France.
1750s	Midwives are replaced by doctors in the American colonies.
1754–63	French and Indian War: Britain acquires almost all French territory in Canada and east of the Mississippi and Florida from Spain.
1755	Mary Jemison, age 12, is captured by Seneca Indians and goes on to live happily with the tribe.
1764	The *Davey v. Turner* decision upholds the joint deed system of conveyance in Pennsylvania, protecting married women's property rights.
1765	With the Stamp Act, Britain imposes the first direct taxation on the American colonies, provoking deep resentment.
1773	The Boston Tea Party: colonists raid British ships in Boston Harbor and throw their cargo of tea overboard. Phillis Wheatley's poetry collection is published.
1774	Britain responds to the Boston Tea Party with the "Intolerable Acts," severely curtailing Massachusetts's powers.
1775	The American War of Independence begins.

Glossary and Further Information

Abenaki A Native American tribe based in New England and Quebec.

Algonquian A family of hundreds of Native American tribes, united by a common language and based on the east coast, Midwest, and Upper West.

almanac A yearly calendar containing important dates.

bastardy The crime of having a child outside wedlock.

bequeath Leave (property) to a person or persons in a will.

broadside Another term for a broadsheet, a large-format newspaper.

chastity The state of refraining from sexual intercourse.

colonize To settle in a country other than one's own.

Creek people Also known as the Muscogee, a Native American people originally from the southeastern United States.

cuckolded Made a cuckold—the husband of an adulteress.

defamation An accusation that damages a person's reputation.

denomination A branch of the Christian Church.

doctrine A set of beliefs.

dower right The right of a widow to inherit one-third of her late husband's estate.

dowry Property or money brought by a bride to her husband on their marriage.

elope Run away. (In modern times, *elope* has come to mean "run away secretly to get married.")

encroachment Intrusion into another person's or people's territory.

excommunicate Officially exclude someone from participation in the sacraments and services of the Christian Church.

executor A person appointed to carry out the terms of another person's will.

feme covert (Anglo-Norman phrase meaning "covered woman") The legal status of a married woman under English common law.

feme sole (Anglo-Norman phrase meaning "single woman") The legal status of an adult, unmarried woman under English common law.

fornication Sexual intercourse between two people not married to each other.

heresy An opinion that goes against the official teachings of the Church.

heretical Describes an opinion that goes against the church's official teachings.

Huron A Native American people, also known as the Wyandot, who were based in the southern part of Ontario, Canada.

Illinois A confederation of Native American tribes, also known as the Illiniwek, based in the upper Mississippi River Valley.

incantation A series of words said as a magic spell or charm.

indentured servant A laborer employed for a fixed term under a contract called an indenture.

indigo A plant grown for its dark blue dye.

infanticide The crime of a mother killing her child within a year of its birth.

intermediary A person who acts as a mediator, interpreter, or link between two people or peoples.

Iroquois A Native American people, also known as the Haudenosaunee ("People of the Longhouse"), who came together to form the Iroquois League, or Confederacy, which originally consisted of five nations. The Iroquois were based in what is now the northeastern United States.

legislature A lawmaking assembly.

malaria A tropical disease.

matrilineal Of or based on kinship with the maternal line.

menopausal Describing a woman who has ceased menstruating.

Miami A Native American tribe originally based in Indiana, southwest Michigan, and Ohio.

Micmac A Native American people based in New England, Canada's Atlantic Provinces, and the Gaspé Peninsula of Quebec.

missionary A person sent on a religious mission, especially one sent to spread or promote Christianity in a foreign country.

nomadic Describes the life of a person, or group of people, who moves from place to place.

Ottawa A Native American people originally based on Manitoulin Island in Lake Huron and in parts of present-day Ontario and Michigan.

pillorying Putting someone in a pillory—a wooden framework with holes for the head and hands, in which an offender was imprisoned and exposed to public abuse.

Puritans A reforming Christian movement of the 16th and 17th centuries.

Quakers The Religious Society of Friends, or Quakers, is a Christian movement founded in the 1650s.

rennet Curdled milk from the stomach of a calf, used to turn milk into cheese.

seizure A sudden attack of illness, such as a stroke or an epileptic fit.

Seneca A Native American nation within the Iroquois Confederacy, originally based in present-day New York.

slander Making a false spoken statement that damages a person's reputation.

tania A tropical plant with edible roots.

testified Gave evidence as a witness in a law court.

theology The study of the nature of God and religious belief.

tomahawk A light ax used as a tool or weapon by Native Americans.

Wampanoag A Native American nation originally based in southeastern Massachusetts and Rhode Island.

BOOKS

Berkin, Carol. *First Generations: Women in Colonial America.* New York: Hill and Wang, 1996.

Bjornlund, Lydia D. *Women in History: Women of Colonial America.* Farmington Hills, MI: Lucent Books, 2004.

Furbee, Mary Rodd. *Outrageous Women of Colonial America.* San Francisco: Jossey Bass, 2001.

Miller, Brandon Marie. *Good Women of a Well-Blessed Land: Women's Lives in Colonial America.* Minneapolis: Lerner Publications, 2003.

Studelska, Jana Voelke. *We the People: Women of Colonial America.* Minneapolis: Compass Point Books, 2007.

Waldrup, Carole Chandler. *More Colonial Women: 25 Pioneers of Early America.* Jefferson, NC: McFarland & Co., 2004.

WEB SITES

http://www.americaslibrary.gov/jb/index.php
http://www.earlyamerica.com
http://www.womenhistoryblog.com

http://www.digitalhistory.uh.edu
http://www.lva.virginia.gov/exhibits/

INDEX

Numbers in **bold** refer to illustrations.

64